To Geoff

Warmest regards +
fond memories of our
Belfast days.

Keith
(KAROVER?)

Bingo, Boggart and the Furry Cube

By the same author

BINGO BONES AND THE BOGGART

Bingo, Boggart and the Furry Cube

K. H. ROBERTS

Illustrated by Val Biro

HODDER AND STOUGHTON
LONDON SYDNEY AUCKLAND TORONTO

To Jean

British Library Cataloguing in Publication Data

Roberts, Keith H.
Bingo, boggart and the furry cube.
I. Title II. Biro, Val
823'.914[J] PZ7

ISBN 0-340-38630-4

First published 1986

Published by Hodder and Stoughton Children's Books, a division of Hodder and Stoughton Ltd, Mill Road, Dunton Green, Sevenoaks, Kent TN13 2YJ

Photoset by Rowland Phototypesetting Ltd, Bury St Edmunds, Suffolk

Printed in Great Britain by T.J. Press (Padstow) Ltd, Padstow, Cornwall

Contents

I

A Funny Place to keep a Friend

'Hurry up or you'll be late!' called Bingo's mum from the bottom of the stairs. 'Come on! Dad's waiting!'

'Coming!' Bingo shouted as he closed the bedroom door and ran down the stairs as fast as he could.

When he reached the bottom step Mum thrust a plastic carrier bag into his hand and after a quick goodbye kiss he rushed into the street where Dad, in his working clothes with his miner's helmet hanging from his belt, was waiting.

''Bye, Mum!' Bingo called, grabbing hold of Dad's outstretched hand. Together they hurried away up the street.

Up the street was the way to the coal mine, or the Pit as Dad called it, and it was also the way to school. Down the street was the way to the sweet shop but on this special day Bingo didn't mind at all that he was going towards school. Today Bingo's class was going on a trip to London and Bingo was going to school earlier than he had ever done in his whole life. After all, he was eight years old.

Bingo counted the doors to the end of his own row of houses. He counted them every day on his way to school and there were always twelve. When he counted them on the way back from school there were always thirteen because then he counted his own door as well. There were twenty-five houses in the row and so, if you were coming up from the sweet shop or down from the school, Bingo's house, in the very middle of the row, was always thirteenth.

When they reached the school Bingo said 'Cheerio!' to Dad and, after carefully looking both ways, ran across the road to his friends who were already waiting in the playground. Dad waved and then walked away to his work at the Pit.

Outside the school gates Bingo hesitated for a moment and gently pulled from his pocket a match-box with a picture of a Sea Captain on the front. Carefully he pushed open the match-box and whispered into it.

'You can be your real self on the train,' he said before closing the box again and slipping it back into his pocket. Bingo smiled and skipped into the school playground where his school friends were waiting.

Now I'm sure you don't keep your best friend in your pocket but Bingo Bones does. Bingo's friend goes almost everywhere with him and seems to enjoy travelling about in this strange way. But today Bingo was setting out on a journey which would be much too long for his friend to spend in a tiny box and that was why he was reminding him that before too long he could be his real self again.

Because of a class topic on famous artists, a trip to London had been arranged to visit a big art gallery and to see the sights. The great day had finally arrived and the whole playground was alive with chatter, but suddenly all was quiet and everyone's eyes turned towards the gate.

The silence was broken as a cheer went up. Miss Simmons, the class teacher, had arrived. Soon the children were all around her to hear the last minute instructions and to make sure that the correct amount of pocket money was written next to their names in Teacher's little book.

Another lady, and a boy of about Bingo's age, arrived at the same time as Miss Simmons. The lady was Mrs Collier, a parent who had volunteered to help out on the trip, and the boy was her son, Alan, who was Bingo's closest friend at school. Alan, or Ally as Bingo called him, came over to Bingo and they planned how they could sit next to each other on the train.

Even though Ally was a good friend, Bingo's very best friend was still in the match-box in his pocket and you can be sure that this friend was not at all like Ally who, even if he had wanted to, could never have climbed into Bingo's pocket, let alone into a match-box. Bingo's other friend was, to say the least, very unusual. He was a Boggart!

And what is a Boggart? Well, Boggart's are distant cousins to the Trolls of Norway and they live in the dark corners of the North. They are even related to the Leprechauns of Ireland, the Piskies of Cornwall and some Boggarts are even related to

Bogey-men but that is one branch of the family that Boggarts seldom talk about.

There are many kinds of Boggart and Bingo's dad had told him all about them. Most Boggarts are quite frightening, and they love to chase after boys and girls. There is the Coal Hole Boggart, the Dark Wood Boggart, the Back Street Boggart and many more besides, but the most frightening of all is the Pit Boggart. He hides round dark corners near the Pit and waits until someone comes along and then . . . well, perhaps we had better not think about that.

'Stay away from the Pit,' Dad would say, 'or the Boggart will get you and then that will be that,' and Bingo did stay away from the Pit until one day, quite accidentally, he disobeyed.

Behind the Pit were three huge grey mountains of waste dust and rock from the Pit and Dad called the mountains the Three Sisters. One day, while chasing a butterfly, Bingo had wandered from the path leading to a stream near the Pit and before he knew it he had found himself at the top of the very tallest of the Three Sisters. There he met Boggart.

Bingo had been very frightened at first but soon he and Boggart became firm friends. They had many adventures together, especially when Bingo found out that, just by imagining, he could change Boggart into whatever shape he wished from the biggest of the big, like a Pit chimney, to the smallest of the small like a caterpillar.

When Boggart was living at home with Bingo he was always in the shape of a caterpillar and Bingo kept him in a big glass jar next to his bed. Sometimes, when no-one was looking, Bingo would close his eyes and imagine as hard as he could and then Boggart would change into his proper self. And what was Boggart like when he was his proper self? Well, now is the time for the rule of wait and see, but for the time being, Boggart was in the shape of a caterpillar, curled up and fast asleep inside the match-box deep in Bingo's pocket. And what sort of a caterpillar was he? He was a Peacock butterfly caterpillar because Peacock caterpillars are furry and whatever else Boggart turned into was also furry. Boggart didn't know why, but that was how it was.

'Come along now!' called Miss Simmons as a coach drew up outside the school gates. 'It's time to go! Line up in twos!'

'This is it, Bingo!' Ally giggled excitedly. 'We're on our way to London!'

2
Travel Trouble

'Come on, you two!' called Mrs Collier from inside an open carriage door. 'You don't want to be left behind, do you?'

'No thanks, Mum,' laughed Ally as he and Bingo climbed on to the train. 'Nobody's going to leave us behind!'

The coach journey from school had taken only a few minutes and now here they were, boarding the train. Quietly and smoothly the big blue and yellow engine pulled its long line of carriages out of the station. In no time at all the trees and houses were flashing past the windows as the big electric train reached full speed. Ally and Bingo had found seats together and, as no-one was sitting opposite to them, they had a table all to themselves. Ally sat next to the window and so Bingo could see straight down the corridor to where a little old man with a gnarled face, a long pointed nose, big ears and twinkly eyes, was sitting all by himself.

The little old man had got on the train at the same time as the children although no-one had seen him come through the ticket-office at the station. This was hardly surprising because when he came through the ticket office he had been hiding in a tiny match-box in a small boy's pocket. The old man was Boggart.

On the station platform everyone had been looking the other way when Bingo had quietly slipped the match-box from his pocket and gently placed a furry caterpillar on a station seat. Walking back to join the rest of his class Bingo had paused for a moment, closed his eyes, and imagined for all he was worth. A little while later an extra passenger boarded the train.

When Boggart was being himself he usually wore a brown woollen shirt, a pair of rough green trousers with yellow patches on the knees and a thick leather belt with a shiny brass buckle. Boggart's favourite piece of clothing was the red and white spotted handkerchief which he wore round his neck.

But Boggart's clothes would have looked a little out of place on a train journey. Everyone would have laughed at his bare feet and some people might have turned their noses up.

And so, Bingo had used his imagination to change Boggart's appearance. The little old man was wearing a brown Norfolk jacket, a dark blue high-necked jumper, a pair of smart green corduroy trousers and a pair of very shiny pointed shoes. Bingo watched as his friend looked down at his feet as though he had never seen shoes there before. And that was the truth of it.

Bingo had never shared his friend with anyone ever since the day he had tried to tell Dad about Boggart and Dad had just laughed. Not even Ally knew about Boggart but Ally had noticed him at the other end of the carriage.

'Look at that funny little man,' said Ally in a quiet voice. Boggart, who was very excited, was looking out of the window and was jerking his head from side to side as he tried to watch the world whizzing by. 'He must think he's at a tennis match. If he isn't careful his head will drop off.'

Bingo started to giggle but stopped immediately as Miss Simmons appeared at his side.

'Here you are,' she said with a smile, dropping a sheaf of papers on to the table. 'I'm glad you're enjoying yourselves but perhaps we can have a little less giggling.'

Miss Simmons moved on to the next group leaving Bingo and Ally to get on with the work sheets which she had just given to them. The work sheets were all about the journey and quite fun to do but a careful eye had to be kept on the passing scenery to answer the questions. Stations had to be ticked off, train numbers collected, bridges and tunnels counted and a lot more besides. Bingo and Ally, who were allowed to work together, took out their pencils and in no time at all the funny little man at the other end of the carriage was forgotten. They worked quietly and the miles rolled by until a voice suddenly made them sit up and look round.

'Tickets please! All tickets, please!' called the voice and Bingo, as he turned, saw the Ticket Inspector standing right behind him.

'Now then, young man,' said the Inspector. 'Who is in charge of you then?'

'Here you are,' called Miss Simmons from further down the carriage. 'I've got the tickets.'

Bingo's face went bright red. He had suddenly realised that he had made a very serious mistake. Boggart didn't have a ticket and when the Inspector found out, as he surely must, Boggart would be thrown off the train at the next station.

3
Boggart makes the Headlines

Bingo had to think as quick as lightning. The Inspector had clicked all the children's tickets and was exchanging a few words with Miss Simmons and Mrs Collier. Any second now he would ask Boggart for his ticket. The man half turned and Bingo, with his heart in his mouth, acted so quickly that his eyes nearly closed with a bang.

Bingo's eyes were so tightly closed that his face wrinkled like a walnut as he imagined as hard as he could. When he had finished he hardly dared look.

One eye opened ever so slightly but it wasn't enough to see properly. Dare he risk it? Bingo took a deep breath and stared wide-eyed down the length of the carriage. There was no sign of Boggart. A huge sigh of relief escaped from Bingo's lips.

'Watch out, Bingo!' Ally said, throwing his arms across the papers on the table. Bingo's sigh had been so strong that everything on the table had been almost blown to the floor.

'Sorry,' apologised Bingo, whose mind was far away from school work. He was too busy watching the Inspector staring at an empty seat and scratching his head. The man spoke to Miss Simmons who also looked at the empty seat and then rubbed her nose with a finger as she always did when she was puzzled. With a final glance and a shrug of his shoulders the Inspector moved on to the next carriage.

Miss Simmons had told the class to remain in their seats and not to wander about the train and so Bingo, even though he was desperate to walk down the carriage, remained where he was and concentrated on his tasks. He and Ally opened their cans of drink and chatted as they worked.

Eventually Bingo's patience ran out. 'I think I'll ask Miss if I can go to the Buffet Car,' Bingo said to his friend. He half rose from his seat and was just saying 'If we get another drink we can keep it until we have our sandwiches,' when the train suddenly began to slow down.

'Too late,' Ally informed Bingo. 'We're here. Look!' Bingo saw that the train was crossing a maze of railway lines and there were engines and trains everywhere. Slowly the end of the platform came into view. Bingo was speechless.

'Come on then, Bingo,' Ally urged his friend. 'We'd better collect our things together. We don't want to be the last off the train, do we?'

Miss Simmons stood up and repeated what Ally had just said about collecting things together. The train came smoothly to a halt and the class was told to stand still until everyone else had left the train. Then, clutching bags and coats, they made their way on to the platform. Bingo made sure he was the last to leave, or at least he thought he was. As he approached the far end of the carriage he stole a quick glance at the seat where Boggart had been sitting. There was nothing there now except a slightly crumpled newspaper and Bingo, as quick as a flash, picked it up and joined his other friends on the station platform.

'Bingo!' exclaimed Mrs Collier. 'You don't need old newspapers for souvenirs.' Mrs Collier, who had been one of the first to leave the train, had walked back along the platform and had entered the carriage again from the other end. Like all grown-ups she was just as much concerned with coats being left behind as she was with enjoying her day out. She had followed Bingo and had seen him pick up the paper. Before Bingo could protest she had whipped it from under his arm and popped it into a bag of litter which she had collected from the train.

Just when he thought he had solved his

problem, poor Bingo found himself with another. Mrs Collier had no idea that the newspaper which she had just taken from Bingo was really Boggart. Bingo just hoped that Ally's mum didn't pay too much attention to it. If she did she might notice that the printing was not black ink but a sort of dark fur in the shape of letters covering each page. She might also notice the front page headlines which read 'BOGGART ARRIVES IN LONDON!'

Fortunately, Mrs Collier didn't have time

to concern herself with a bag of litter. She was far too busy helping Miss Simmons with the children who were moving down the platform in a long crocodile. Miss Simmons was at the front of the line, Mrs Collier was at the back and Bingo kept close to Ally's mum. Bingo looked for a litter bin so that he could offer to put the bag of rubbish in and perhaps rescue the furry newspaper, but there wasn't a bin to be seen. Bingo then had second thoughts, for he knew that if Mrs Collier hung on to the bag until they had passed the Ticket Collector, the problem of Boggart not having a ticket would be solved.

The class buzzed with excitement as Miss Simmons led the way up the slope at the end of the platform. She handed in the tickets and the group was gathered together in the station hall where all heads were counted. Then Miss Simmons led the children to where a huge red circle with a line through it showed the entrance to the Underground. Bingo began to worry, and found it hard to listen to

Ally who was chattering non-stop about the biggest station he had ever seen and about how many people there were and how he didn't know any of them.

'Here you are, Bingo,' said Mrs Collier as they walked towards the Underground. She held out a plastic bag. 'Pop this into the litter bin over there, and no old newspapers, thank you.'

With a smile on his face Bingo grabbed the bag and ran to the bin. He smiled even more when he reached the bin and saw that it was nearly full. Carefully placing the bag so that the newspaper was sticking up over the edge of the bin he raced back and joined the line of children disappearing down the steps leading to the trains. As he reached the steps he glanced back to the bin. Yes, there was the paper still sticking up over the edge. For a brief second he closed his eyes, bumped into Ally and, still smiling, followed the class.

4
Seeing the Sights

It was just as well that Bingo didn't see the results of his imagining. He would never have kept from giggling. People were most surprised to see a funny little man, covered in litter, emerge from a litter bin. Surely, Boggart was the strangest jack-in-the-box ever, especially as he was wearing the uniform of a station porter.

'What on earth are the railways coming to?' exclaimed an old lady as she hurried away from the scene.

Bingo glanced over his shoulder and, each time he turned a corner in the tunnels leading to the Underground, he caught a glimpse of Boggart following behind. Bump! Once again, instead of looking where he was going, Bingo crashed into Ally, who, with the rest of the class, had stopped while Miss Simmons bought tickets.

'No pushing, now!' Miss Simmons said as several other children bumped into each other. Bingo said nothing. He was aware of someone standing behind him and he knew that it was Boggart.

Bingo had been rather clever in his imagining. He knew that if Boggart was dressed like a railway worker then he would not need a ticket. Boggart walked through with the class and watched in surprise as the children disappeared down a long sloping hole.

'Don't worry,' Bingo whispered. 'It's only an escalator.'

At the bottom of the moving staircase, Miss Simmons and Mrs Collier were counting heads again. Bingo was the last of the children but behind him came several other people. One of them was a porter and when Miss Simmons saw him her eyes nearly popped out of her head. She couldn't help staring at the man who looked so much like . . . Miss Simmons did a lot of nose rubbing.

The children waited on the platform as the

train rumbled out of the tunnel. Chattering like monkeys they climbed on board and the train zoomed away through the tunnel at the other end of the platform. 'Isn't this fun?' whispered Boggart who had found his way to Bingo's side.

'Shhhhhh!' Bingo whispered in return.

The train finally arrived at Piccadilly Circus and Boggart followed the children until they emerged once more into daylight. When they all saw the Tourist Bus which

would take them round the sights they felt excited enough to burst.

Bingo wondered how he could get Boggart on to the bus but there wasn't time for imagining as Miss Simmons said 'Hurry along, please! I've already booked the tickets. Upstairs! Three to a seat!'

Ally's mum went first as Miss Simmons counted the children. Boggart had joined the queue and just as Miss Simmons was about to count Bingo as number twenty-five, Bingo had an idea.

'After you, Miss,' he said. 'Ladies before gentlemen.'

'Thank you!' Miss Simmons said and climbed the stairs. The conductor was about to ask Boggart for his ticket when Bingo turned round.

'He's with us,' said Bingo truthfully.

'Sorry, Sir,' said the conductor to Boggart who grinned all over his face. He had never been called 'Sir' before.

Like most eight-year-olds, Bingo liked a

bit of mischief and when his funny friend was half way up the stairs Bingo closed his eyes and allowed his imagination to take over. Boggart never felt a thing and continued to the top step and along the bus. Still chuckling to himself, Bingo scrambled after his friend and sat near the back, next to Ally and David Bowker, another friend.

Miss Simmons, sitting near the front, stood up after allowing a city gent to squeeze past to the seat in front of her. 'Sit still and listen,' she ordered. 'We're almost ready to go. Keep your eyes open and at the end of the trip stay in your seats until I tell you to move.'

Miss Simmons sat down as the bus moved off. Bingo, Ally and David enjoyed the trip and held a competition to see how many famous places they could see before Miss Simmons pointed them out. Bingo got the Houses of Parliament, the Tower of London and St Paul's Cathedral. Ally got Big Ben, Trafalgar Square and Westminster Abbey while David was the first to see Tower Bridge, Nelson's Column and Buckingham Palace. They saw lots of other famous places but with the score at three each the trip finally came to an end.

Miss Simmons waited until everyone else had left the bus before she stood up to give the class permission to leave. She was about to speak when she noticed that the city gent had not moved.

'Excuse me!' she said, tapping the man on the shoulder, 'but we are waiting until everyone else is off. Please don't wait for us.'

'Thank you,' said the man in the pin-striped suit and the bowler hat. 'Very kind of you!' he said most politely.

Miss Simmons smiled until the man turned round to look at her and then her face went white, and she started to rub her nose again.

Bingo saw what was happening and almost laughed out loud as Boggart winked at him on his way to the stairs. Poor Miss Simmons. She looked very puzzled and Bingo hoped that she wouldn't rub her nose completely off.

It took Miss Simmons several minutes to recover before she could lead the class to St James's Park where they were to have their picnic lunch.

5
Atten–shun!!!

'Come along, now!' Miss Simmons called and everyone put their lunch boxes away and picked up their litter. The picnic had been super and the ducks, geese, pigeons, sparrows and pelicans in St James's Park had enjoyed the treat of crumbs and crisps which the class had shared with them.

The line of children walked along the tree-lined path and on leaving the park Teacher saw everyone across the road. 'There are lots of things to see,' she said, 'but we haven't time to stop at them all. Stay close and follow me!'

Bingo and Ally followed the class to Horse Guards Parade. The boys marched along like soldiers and Bingo, through the corner of his eye, saw a funny little man following at a distance. He was also marching and he looked most odd.

The class next passed through an archway into Whitehall and then halted in surprise. There, mounted on horseback was a tall Guardsman. His scarlet tunic was as smart as could be, his long black boots were polished to perfection and his shiny breastplate shone like silver. Ally and Bingo were quite speechless.

'Look!' said Ally when at last he found his voice. 'Look at his hat!' The Guardsman wore a shiny silver and gold helmet with a tall horse-hair plume. By his side hung a long sword.

The children grinned when some tourists tried to make the soldier smile by pulling faces and telling funny stories but the Guardsman never moved. His face was as still as a rock and his eyes stared steadily ahead.

Bingo felt a tug on his sleeve and turned to see Boggart smiling cheekily. Boggart shot a glance first at the Guardsman and then at Bingo who knew instantly what his friend meant. Boggart drifted back into the crowd.

Bingo wondered what to do. He knew what Boggart wanted but surrounded by crowds of people he knew that it wouldn't be easy. Bingo even wondered whether or not it was a good idea, but there again it wasn't often that his friend actually asked to be changed into something. Bingo turned his head and squinted sideways at Boggart before briefly closing his eyes.

'I'll bet you can't make him laugh,' said Ally, interrupting Bingo's thoughts and pointing at the Guardsman.

I bet I can, thought Bingo before answering. 'I don't think Miss would be very pleased if we tried,' he said. 'She'll tell us off for being silly.'

Ally looked at Miss Simmons whose eyes were fixed firmly on the children. 'I think you're right,' said Bingo's friend, 'but it would be fun to try.'

Bingo simply nodded in agreement.

'I wonder if they have to sit in front of a

mirror for weeks on end, practising not laughing?' Ally continued.

Bingo laughed at the thought of it. 'I wouldn't last a minute,' he said but Ally didn't hear. His attention had shifted back to the soldier and everyone else seemed to be looking in the same direction. Something was happening and, at first, neither Bingo nor Ally could work out what it was.

The soldier's face was now nearly the same colour as his tunic and his eyes were moist. Ally thought that the Guardsman was going to cry but Bingo knew otherwise. The soldier was trying not to laugh. His cheeks twitched, his shoulders shook gently and every now and then he had to blink to clear the tears from his eyes. He sniffled and snuffled and sometimes made a sort of choking noise. Some tourists who were standing close by thought that their efforts to amuse the man had finally been rewarded but once again Bingo knew differently.

Poor Guardsman. His face was now deep

purple as he twisted his nose, his eyebrows, his mouth and, underneath his helmet even his ears wiggled. Tears rolled down his face and beads of sweat formed on his brow as he fought hard to stop his chuckle bubble bursting.

Suddenly Bingo felt sorry for the Guardsman, who was looking more and more uncomfortable every minute. The crowd knew that he was laughing but little did they realise what he was laughing at. If they had only turned round and looked back across the road they would have known immediately. Bingo turned and looked but he knew what he would see.

On the other side of the road was another soldier. He was smaller than the laughing Guardsman and not quite so smart. His shirt tail was hanging out from under the back of his tunic, his helmet was tipped to one side, his trousers were four sizes too big and instead of a sword he carried a long stick of rhubarb which still had a huge leaf attached.

Not only did the soldier look funny but he was also doing a funny hopping, marching, skipping jumping walk, sometimes standing up as tall as he could and at other times bending low so that his chin nearly touched the ground. The real Guardsman, because he was on horseback, could see this copy of himself over the heads of the tourists. Even Bingo laughed out loud when he caught sight of Boggart's antics.

Bingo knew that he had to do something, and so he waited until a big red bus was nearly level with Boggart and then he closed his eyes and imagined. When the bus had gone by the funny soldier had disappeared and a little old man stood at the kerb, looking across at the crowd.

Ally nudged Bingo. 'He's stopped now,' he whispered, 'but wasn't it a laugh.'

'It was,' said Bingo although he was talking about something completely different.

Miss Simmons had tears in her eyes too but she tried to keep her face straight as she said 'That's enough of that. Let's be moving along to the art gallery now.'

Bingo and Ally were still giggling ten minutes later when, on reaching the River Thames, Teacher called another halt to count heads.

6
Works of Art

Miss Simmons had done a lot of Art with her class and one day David Bowker had said that his dad had told him about an art gallery in London which had paid a fortune for a pile of bricks. Miss Simmons had smiled and promised that when they went to London they would visit a real art gallery. Now, with the picnic lunch over, here they were walking in through the entrance to The Tute Gallery.

Miss Simmons led the way through the huge rooms and the children stared open-mouthed at the strange figures. Bingo stared over his shoulder to see if *he* could see a strange figure. Yes, there he was in the next room. Bingo closed his eyes.

Boggart's cracked old grin broke out again when he realised what had happened. He was now dressed as a Gallery Attendant.

Bingo turned his attention to what Miss Simmons was saying. She was talking about the various pieces of sculpture and telling the children to look for interesting shapes. Everyone giggled when she pointed to an exhibit made out of old pieces of machinery. It really did look as though it would have been much more at home on the back of a rag and bone man's cart.

After talking for another few minutes, Miss Simmons told the class to go off in twos to explore for themselves and to meet by the entrance in an hour. Bingo and Ally wandered off to see what they could find.

The two friends spent some time gazing and giggling their way around several rooms until Ally decided that he would like to buy some postcards from the Gallery shop. Bingo preferred looking at the pictures and so they agreed that Ally should go off on his own and meet Bingo in ten minutes.

A rather small sized Gallery Attendant had been following the boys and when

Ally disappeared he approached Bingo.

'Phew!' Boggart gasped. 'I barely know where I am. I've hardly had a chance to speak to you all day, but it is exciting. Isn't it?'

'It is!' agreed Bingo. 'And it isn't over yet.'

'You're right!' Boggart replied and then, with a sideways glance, said 'Look out! Here comes trouble!'

Into the far end of the room had walked a real Gallery Attendant. If he saw Boggart's face he would know immediately that Bingo's friend was an imposter.

'Quick! Follow me!' Bingo exclaimed and shuffled across the floor into the next room.

'Have we lost him yet?' Boggart asked. Bingo didn't answer. He set off again for the door at the other end of the room, stooping low and dodging between the statues. Boggart, bent low like a waddling duck, followed behind.

'I think he's spotted us,' whispered Bingo as Boggart joined him behind a huge stone sculpture full of holes. Bingo peeped

through one of the lower holes and was quite shocked to see the Attendant standing on the other side. Scrambling to their feet the two friends slid into the next room but the man was quickly after them. They dodged from room to room but still the man in the uniform followed in pursuit. Most of the rooms in the Gallery had two doors and so it was quite easy for the small boy and his friend to keep ahead.

Suddenly Bingo saw Miss Simmons coming in the opposite direction. He dodged into a room and she didn't see him but Boggart was not so lucky. Miss Simmons could hardly believe her eyes. She rubbed her nose very hard and looked extremely puzzled. Then she turned to Mrs Collier, who had seen nothing of what had happened.

The minute she turned Boggart dived into the room with Bingo and they flattened their backs against the wall just inside the door. They both looked hot and bothered. Bingo peeped round the door and sighed one of his deepest sighs as he saw Mrs Collier and Miss Simmons walking away.

'You said that London was an exciting place,' his funny friend said.

They strolled towards the door but then stopped in their tracks. They had forgotten about the Attendant and now there he was, heading straight for them. Rushing back into the small room Bingo headed for the other door but once again stopped dead. This room only had one door and the Attendant would walk through it at any second.

'Sorry, Boggart,' Bingo gasped. 'There's only one thing for it!' He closed his eyes and made his imagination work as hard as it could.

'Hello there, young man,' said the Attendant as he came through the door. 'Is everything all right?'

'Errr, yes!' Bingo replied, although his cheeks felt very hot.

'Good!' said the man, peering round the room. 'You haven't seen one of my friends in here, have you? I thought I saw him come this way.'

'No, I haven't,' Bingo replied honestly.

The man turned to leave but then spun on his heels. He took off his cap and wiped his brow. 'How on earth did that get there?' he asked.

Bingo turned to look although he knew what he would see. In the middle of the room stood a huge green furry cube with a sign saying DO NOT TOUCH. At that very moment another Attendant walked in and he too looked quite shocked by the big bright green cube.

'What's this then, Jack?' he asked. 'When did that come in?'

'Dunno, Bert,' the first Attendant replied. 'They usually let us know if there's any change in the displays.'

'I'll find out,' Jack said. 'Keep an eye on it until I get back.' As he disappeared an old lady and gentleman entered.

'Marvellous!' exclaimed the old man, staring at the cube.

'Wonderful!' his wife agreed in such a high voice that people in nearby rooms came flocking in to see what all the fuss was about.

Someone said it was the best thing they had ever seen and a lot of others agreed. As the crowd grew, Bingo was almost crushed between all the people fighting to get a better view. Soon the room was so full that no-one else could squeeze in.

Above the chatter and bustle a voice was

heard. 'Excuse me please!' it said. 'Please let me through!'

The Attendant who had gone off to find out what it was all about pushed his way through, bringing with him an important looking gentleman. Someone said that he was the Director of the Gallery.

The Director squeezed in and stared in complete silence at the cube. Obviously he knew nothing at all about it but, as it was attracting so much attention, he thought that

he had better make the best of it. He stood on a bench and addressed the crowd.

'I am pleased to see the interest which you have shown in our most recent work,' he began, 'and I am sure you will appreciate that we always try to find the most modern sculpture. This,' he said, pointing at the cube, 'is displayed at The Tute for the first time today.'

Bingo, who had been watching the proceedings with growing alarm, felt someone tug at the back of his trousers. He looked round to see Ally crawling through the legs of the people at the front.

'Here you are!' Ally said with relief. 'Miss Simmons and my mum are looking everywhere for you.'

'Shhhhh!' Bingo whispered with a finger to his lips. 'I'm listening!'

Ally stood by Bingo's side as the Director carried on with his speech. He was amazed that Bingo was so interested, for he couldn't understand a word of what was being said.

Neither could Bingo but he was only trying to stay near Boggart, who was now a furry cube, for as long as possible.

At the end of the speech everyone clapped and the Director, still looking bemused, climbed down and forced his way out of the room. Everyone congratulated him and patted him on the back and by the time he reached the door he was wearing a satisfied smile.

The crowd thinned out a little and Bingo caught sight of Miss Simmons beckoning from near the door. With Ally leading, they wandered over to join the other children.

'It will soon be time to leave,' Miss Simmons informed them. 'Come along now, Bingo and Alan.'

Bingo went white with panic. He hadn't realised that time had passed so quickly. He had even forgotten about meeting his friend. Ally had waited for ten minutes before going off to find Bingo and that was when he bumped into Miss Simmons. Bingo knew he couldn't change Boggart with lots of people watching. He didn't know what to do.

'Please, Miss Simmons,' Bingo pleaded, 'can we have a quick look at this new thing. The man said it was new today. Please, Miss!'

Miss Simmons looked at her watch. 'Very well!' she said. 'But we mustn't be too long.' Bingo knew that this would be his last chance. He crossed his fingers and hoped that he could be last out of the room.

While they were admiring the cube the Director returned with a photographer who started taking photographs from all angles. Boggart was certainly the centre of attraction now!

Bingo was looking worried as he glanced this way and that, wishing everyone out of the room, but there was absolutely nothing he could do.

The final piece of magic was not to be and when Miss Simmons said 'Come on! Time to go!' Bingo knew that it was all over.

7
News

Bingo slept fitfully that night. The journey home had been very tiring, and nearly all the children had fallen asleep on the train. Bingo thought that the journey was more like a nightmare for, when the train pulled out of Euston Station and away from London, he had hidden his face deep inside the hood of his anorak. Ally thought that his friend had gone to sleep but Bingo was simply hiding his tears.

All the way home Bingo's thoughts had been full of 'If only . . .' and 'Poor Boggart!' No matter how hard he tried, Bingo could not think of a way to return to London to save his friend. Perhaps, he thought, when he was a man, he would go back to The Tute Gallery and imagine his friend back into his proper shape. But would the magic work when he was older? There didn't seem to be a lot of magic in the lives of the grown-ups he knew.

Dreams tormented his sleep and things were no easier when Mum popped her head round the bedroom door and reminded him that it was time to get ready for school. The first thing Bingo saw when he opened his eyes was the big glass jar at the side of his bed where Boggart usually lived. Bingo hoped that losing Boggart had just been a nightmare and he sat upright and stared at the jar. Except for a few tiny crumbs of coal, put there by Bingo for his friend to eat, the jar was completely empty.

'Not feeling well?' Mum asked as she stared at Bingo over the breakfast table. 'You look as though you're sickening for something.'

Bingo didn't feel too good at all but there was no sense in making a scene. 'I'm all right,' he said, trying to sound as cheerful as possible.

'Perhaps,' said Mum, pouring Bingo a cup

of tea, 'you're tired after all the excitement of yesterday. You haven't told me about it yet. You were nearly asleep when we met you off the coach.'

Even though Bingo was feeling quite miserable he couldn't let Mum know and so he told the story, as cheerfully as possible and missing out the bits about Boggart, of his day out in London.

Mum was quite impressed with all the things that Bingo had seen because she had never been to London. She said that she would like to go and this filled Bingo with hope but his hope was short-lived.

'There are lots of places I would like to see,' Mum said with a far away look in her eyes, 'but I don't suppose I'll see any of them until you've grown up a bit.' Bingo wondered how much growing he needed to do.

Mum started to tidy the table and when Bingo had finished his breakfast he picked up the newspaper. His eyes nearly popped out of his head when he looked at the front page for there, staring out at him, was a picture of the Cube. The headline above the picture said

'ROW OVER SCULPTURE'

and the report under the picture said that the Cube was at the centre of a big argument. Some people said it was wonderful while others said it was nothing more than an overgrown cushion. Bingo read the report over and over again until Mum reminded him that it was time for school.

'You can take the paper with you,' Mum said when Bingo showed her the picture and told her how they had seen the strange object in the photograph. 'But make sure you bring it back again this afternoon so that Dad can read it.'

Bingo promised to return the paper and, after gathering his things together and shouting ''Bye,' to Mum, went out through the front door. Bingo usually skipped all the way to school but this morning his feet felt like lead. He patted the empty match-box in

his pocket and thought about his friend, hundreds of miles away. He hoped that Boggart wouldn't be too lonely.

School came and went. Bingo found that the harder he worked the faster time went by and so he put all his efforts into his work. He answered questions about the trip, did some writing and drew a super picture of the Tower of London.

At the end of the day the whole classroom was covered with pictures of the trip. Bingo was sorry when school was over, for it meant that once more he was left with nothing but his own thoughts.

Dad had arrived home before Bingo and he found that talking to him helped a lot. Dad was interested in everything Bingo had done and seen and then Grandad, who lived next door, came in and so Bingo had to tell the whole story over again. Grandad told Bingo about the time that he had been to London to the Rugby Final and how he had got himself lost on the Underground. Bingo laughed and felt a lot better.

'Hello there, young man,' said Mum as she came in from her work at the cotton mill. 'You look a lot brighter than this morning.'

'Of course he does,' said Grandad. 'Talking to all us young folk has cheered him up!'

Everyone laughed, and soon they were sitting down to tea. Grandad kept asking Bingo about the trip and Bingo went over and over it again. After tea, Dad settled down with the newspaper, which Bingo had remembered to bring home from school, and Grandad switched on the television to watch the news. Bingo lay on the rug and thumbed through the pages of a comic.

Grandad suddenly sat upright in his chair. 'Look, Bingo!' he exclaimed. 'They're talking about that funny old block which you said you'd seen.'

'They were talking about that at the Pit,' Dad said from behind his newspaper. 'I can't see what all the fuss is about.'

'I don't know what the world's coming

to,' Mum agreed. 'They'll be putting jars of jam in the art galleries next.'

Grandad laughed and sucked at his empty pipe. 'You're right,' he said, 'but let Bingo listen to what they're saying. He picked the right day to go to London, didn't he?'

Bingo recognized the picture of the Tute Gallery and he shouted 'I've seen him!' when the Director appeared on the screen. The Director refused to say who had created the big green cube and Bingo knew why because he himself was the only person in the whole wide world who could answer that question.

The picture on the screen shifted from the Director and then there, as large as life, was the famous Cube. Bingo stared hard and watched as the object was shown in close-up. All the time the Cube was in view the Director was talking, although Bingo wasn't paying much attention to the words. However, the Director's last words on the matter struck Bingo's ears with the force of an explosion.

' . . . and,' continued the Director, 'its fame has already spread around the world. Only two hours ago I received a telephone call from a museum in New York and they have offered half a million dollars for this fine work of art. We shall find it very difficult to refuse this amazing offer.'

The news ended and Bingo was once again in deep despair. If Boggart was sold to America he would never ever see him again.

8

. . . and more News

Bingo slept better that night, not because he was any less worried, but because he was so exhausted with worry that he collapsed on to his pillow and didn't stir again until Mum came to wake him next morning.

'Come on, Sunshine!' she called through the open door. 'There's another picture of your famous Cube in the paper.'

Bingo was out of bed, washed and dressed in a flash and down at the breakfast table quicker than he had ever been before.

'My goodness!' Mum exclaimed as she poured the tea. 'You're a regular little whirlwind this morning.'

Bingo forced a smile and glanced across at the newspaper which lay open on the table. There was nothing new; just another picture of the Cube but with the Director standing beside it and an article about the offer from

America which Bingo didn't even bother to read. He wished he could imagine Boggart into something just by looking at the picture but that was impossible.

Bingo set off for school a few minutes later and still he didn't skip. He didn't even have his match-box.

Miss Simmons was full of the news from The Tute. How lucky they had been, she said, to have been at the place where an important piece of news had happened. Bingo didn't think they had been at all lucky. He just sat and looked miserable.

'And I'm sure,' Miss Simmons said, 'that some of you will be making another journey next weekend with your parents. At least I hope so. Anyone who has read the newspaper this morning will know what I mean.'

'I do!' David called out. 'My Dad says he can't wait to see the the Cube. He says he's going to buy it to put his feet up on after work.'

Bingo's ears pricked up. What was all this

about something in the newspaper? He began to wish he had read the article next to the picture but his wishes only lasted for a minute until Miss Simmons produced her own newspaper. She held it up and pointed to the picture.

'This is good news!' Miss Simmons continued. 'As you can see, the Cube will not be going to America after all. The Director of The Tute Gallery has had so many letters from people who want to see it that he thinks the Cube ought to remain here. It will go on tour to Birmingham, Belfast, Edinburgh, Bristol and Liverpool but it starts its tour next Saturday at . . .'

'Manchester!' David called out.

'Well done!' responded Miss Simmons. 'It will come to Manchester first!'

Bingo couldn't believe his ears. Could this really be true?

The more Bingo listened to Teacher the more excited he became. He wondered if there was any chance of him seeing Boggart again. Would Dad, or even Grandad take him to the Gallery in Manchester? He would even offer a year's pocket money if only someone would take him.

Bingo tingled with excitement and when Miss Simmons had finished talking about the exhibition he couldn't wait to start work.

Miss Simmons reminded everyone that Parents' Evening was coming up soon and she said that she wanted a really good display. She asked the class to continue with the London project and then she went round to each boy and girl to see how they were getting on.

The project continued in the afternoon and Miss Simmons came to look at Bingo's work. 'I've done my writing,' Bingo said, 'and you've marked it all. I think I need to do some more pictures.'

'You're right!' said teacher. 'I'm sure that with your imagination you can do something special. We've nearly got a wall full of Big Bens and Nelson's Columns.'

A rather strange smile grew on Bingo's lips. 'I think I can,' he said. 'I really think I can.'

Miss Simmons nodded and went on to David and Ally who were also drawing pictures.

When it was nearly home time Miss Simmons started to call out each member of the class to show their work to everyone else. Bingo watched as each child in turn walked out to the front of the class and everyone clapped for the pictures. Bingo was last. He waited patiently until Teacher called his name.

'Bingo!' called Miss Simmons at last. 'I've left you until the end because I haven't heard a peep from you all day. I'm sure you've got something special for us to look at.'

Bingo held his paper close to him then no-one could see what was on it until the last minute. He walked to Miss Simmons' desk and she stared as Bingo held his picture high.

Everyone giggled. Along the top it said

'Interesting people I saw on our trip,' and there, staring out at everyone, were four very funny people. They were beautifully drawn but the strange thing about them was that they all had the same faces.

Miss Simmons' eyes opened wide as she stared at the figures. She could hardly believe what she saw. There was the funny little old man from the train, a railway porter, a city gent and an attendant from The Tute Gallery. They were all sitting on top of a big green cube.

Bingo smiled to himself when he looked at Miss Simmons. She was rubbing her nose again.

'Miss!' Sandra called out. 'They've all got the same faces. You can't have four people who all look alike. Can you?'

Miss Simmons blinked. It was as though she found the pictures hard to believe. 'I think you sometimes can,' she said. 'I think you sometimes can.' She blinked again and thought deeply while the class watched silently. Then she rubbed her nose again.

A few minutes later class was dismissed and everyone ran out into the playground. Bingo's eyes lit up when he saw Grandad waiting for him at the gate.

'Hello there, young man,' said Grandad as Bingo rushed up to him. 'You look a bit more cheerful. Your mum said you weren't very happy this morning so I thought we'd have a visit to the sweet shop to cheer you up. It looks as though we won't need to go after all.'

In spite of Grandad's teasing, they did visit the sweet shop and Mrs Molly, who owned the shop, was soon measuring out Bingo's favourite sweets; a quarter of Mint Balls. Grandad told Mrs Molly that Bingo hadn't been too happy over the last couple of days.

'You mustn't come in here looking miserable,' Mrs Molly said. 'You'll turn all my sweets bad and make the Jelly Babies cry. Then I'll have to sell the shop.'

The sweets were shared as Bingo and Grandad walked back up the street towards home and soon they were going in through Bingo's front door.

'Come on, Bingo!' shouted Dad. 'Tell me what you think about the news.'

'I haven't told him yet,' said Grandad. 'I thought I'd let you tell him. After all, it was your idea.'

Bingo bounded into the kitchen where Dad was enjoying a cup of tea.

'Well, Bingo,' said Dad as Bingo climbed on to his lap. 'You've made so much fuss about this Cube of yours that I'd like to see it for myself. How would you like to come to Manchester on Saturday?'

For the first time in his life, Bingo was stuck for words.

9
Where's Grandad?

Once again Bingo and Ally sat next to each other on the train. After the longest few days Bingo could ever remember they were off to see the Cube. There was no funny little man at the end of the carriage this time but there was Ally, who had been invited on the outing, Grandad, and Bingo's mum and dad.

'It's a good job we started early,' said Dad. 'It will be very busy today. Everyone at the Pit was talking about the Cube and there are lots of people going to see it.'

'The early bird catches the worm,' said Grandad, twiddling his favourite walking stick.

'Or the caterpillar!' thought Bingo, hopefully patting the empty match-box in his pocket.

The train journey was only about half an hour and soon they were stepping out on to the platform of the big station. Ally and Bingo helped Grandad down the step and, after a few minutes walk, they were standing outside the Gallery.

Bingo and Ally skipped up to the notice on the front doors and called out 'Ten o'clock. They open at ten o'clock. What time is it now?'

Grandad fished his gold watch out of his pocket and flipped open the front. 'Quarter to nine,' he announced after squinting at the fingers. 'We've a long wait yet.'

'Then I think I'll have a quick look round the shops,' said Mum. 'You can save me a place in the queue if it gets busy.'

'And I could do with some tobacco,' said Grandad, peering into his empty pouch.

'I'll stay with the art experts,' Dad offered. 'Don't be too long!'

Mum trotted off in one direction and Grandad went off in another. Dad and the two boys stood outside the big doors and waited. Other people started to arrive and a

queue began to form which, in twenty minutes, stretched round the corner and out of sight.

With about ten minutes to go before the Gallery opened, Mum arrived back armed with various shopping bags. She put down the bags and gasped: 'Well, that's the weekend shopping done, but where's Grandad?'

'He hasn't come back yet,' said Dad. 'I

hope he hasn't got lost!'

'He won't get lost,' Mum replied. 'He knows Manchester like the back of his hand. He's probably found someone to talk to. You know what he's like. He'll talk to anyone and he always forgets the time.'

'Look!' interrupted Bingo. 'They're starting to open the doors.'

A man in uniform was pushing open the big doors. 'We'll let a few of you in,' said the man. 'Go straight through, follow the signs and wait outside the other doors.'

'What about your grandad?' Ally asked.

'He'll have the sense to wait for us if we're not here,' said Dad. 'We can meet up with him later.'

'I do hope he'll be all right,' Mum said uneasily as they walked into the huge hall.

Following the signs which said 'To THE CUBE' Bingo, Mum, Dad and Ally walked through the corridors lined with paintings and statues until they arrived at another set of doors which were still locked. Looking back every now and then, along the line of people in the queue behind them, they tried to see Grandad but there was still no sign of him.

'Do you think your famous Cube's in there?' Dad asked as Bingo peered at the locked doors.

Bending down to peer through the brass keyhole, Bingo was worrying as much about Grandad as he was about the Cube. 'I don't know,' he replied. 'I can't see it. There's someone standing at the other side of the door.' Bingo could just make out the back of an Attendant's coat.

'It seems like a lot of fuss about nothing!' said Mum who was also worrying about Grandad. 'I'd much rather see Grandad than that furry block.'

Bingo wanted to see both Grandad and the Cube. He knew that he stood a good chance of being first in the room and that would give him the opportunity to work some quick magic, but he also wanted to see that Grandad was all right. He tried to imagine where Grandad might be and that was where he made his mistake.

Bingo peeped again through the keyhole, still trying to imagine what Grandad had got up to, when the attendant on the other side of the door moved to one side. There, at the other end of the room Bingo suddenly saw what he had come to see. There was the Cube!

Bingo hadn't expected to see the Cube and, unfortunately, he was still imagining what Grandad was doing. Suddenly, the Cube wasn't there any more, but Grandad was. Bingo had accidentally imagined Boggart into the shape of Grandad.

Bingo quickly started to imagine Boggart into something else, perhaps even back into the Cube, but he was too late. The Attendant moved again and Bingo's view was blocked.

A loud shout of 'Hey! You! What do you think you're doing in here?' came from the other side of the doors and Bingo stood back as the doors were flung open.

The crowd surged forwards but the Attendant stretched out his arms. 'You can't come in!' he said. There's a bit of a problem.'

The Attendant locked the doors behind him and ran off down the corridor while the crowd murmured.

'I wonder what's going on?' Mum asked as the Attendant, along with several other Attendants, reappeared. They looked very stern.

Unlocking the room again they marched in but this time they left the doors open. Bingo, Mum, Dad and Ally peeped round the door to see what was happening.

The men walked quickly through the room towards an old man who was sitting calmly on a display stand, underneath which was a sign saying THE CUBE.'

'Oh dear!' thought Bingo. 'Now I've really done it. All these people have come to see the Cube and it isn't here any more, and what's worse is that somewhere about the building there are two Grandads!'

10
Priceless

Bingo didn't have much time to worry, not after Mum peeped through the door and saw what she thought was Grandad. She wasn't at all happy when the men walked straight up to him and started to take him out through a side door.

'That's my father!' she shouted. 'Hey! Stop! Where are you taking him?'

One of the Attendants turned back and came to the door. 'I'm sorry,' he said, 'but it looks as though the exhibition will be cancelled. You had all better go home.'

The people in the queue mumbled unhappily and started to leave.

'But that's my father in there,' Mum said earnestly. 'Why are those men taking him away? I can't go home without him!'

The Attendant looked at Mum and said in a kindly voice, 'Well, Madam, I think you

had better come along too. We have a slight problem and we think your father might be able to help us sort it out.'

'We're all coming!' said Dad and they all followed the man who followed the men who had taken away the man they thought was Bingo's Grandad. But he wasn't!!!

'Sit down there, please,' said the Attendant. 'We'll try not to keep you long.'

They had been led into a corridor which

was lined on one side with offices. Each office had a window on to the corridor and through one of them they could see 'Grandad' talking to an important-looking gentleman and the attendants.

'I do hope he hasn't done anything silly!' said Mum. 'You know what he's like sometimes.'

No-one replied. They just stared as 'Grandad' talked to the men. They couldn't hear what was being said but as time went by the men looked less severe and one or two of them had even started to smile. After a few more minutes one of the men even made him a cup of tea and soon they were all smiling.

'Grandad' caught sight of Bingo and everyone else through the window and they exchanged waves. Bingo was feeling better but he was still worried that the real Grandad would appear at any second. Then he would have an awful lot of explaining to do.

Soon, the men who were talking to 'Grandad' moved away from him and started to talk in a huddle and one of them came out to explain that everything was all right and that they wouldn't keep them waiting much longer. When he went back into the office he didn't make a very good job of closing the door and Bingo, who was becoming a little agitated again, stood up. Leaning on the wall by the door he could just hear what the men, in hushed voices, were saying.

'Nobody knows how the Cube got in The Tute anyway. We can just say it disappeared as mysteriously as it arrived.'

'But people don't know that it's a mystery. Perhaps we ought to make another one and just put it in the old one's place.'

'Good idea. I'll get my Missus to buy some green fur-fabric and she can have it ready for Monday morning. She's a dab hand at making soft toys. Settled?'

'Settled!' agreed everyone in the office, including 'Grandad' who wasn't supposed to be listening.

'Good!' said the important looking

gentleman loudly so that 'Grandad' and everyone in the corridor could hear. 'Then I'll just go and put up a notice saying that the exhibition is cancelled due to technical reasons and will now open on Monday morning.'

Everyone nodded in agreement and one of the attendants brought 'Grandad' out into the corridor. 'Sorry to have detained you,' said the Attendant, 'but we've had a few problems and we thought that your father could help us. No doubt he will explain it all to you later.'

Boggart winked at Bingo but didn't speak.

'No use hanging around then,' said Mum. 'We'd better be off home. Come along, Grandad.'

Mum led the way and Dad and Ally followed behind. Bingo grabbed 'Grandad's' sleeve and held him back. He wasn't going to lose the chance.

Bingo looked for an opportunity to

change Boggart into something else but everywhere they went in the Gallery there were people about. He was still a little worried, because if Mum and Dad decided to go straight home it might mean that the real Grandad was left behind and he couldn't think of a way out of that problem.

They reached the Gallery entrance and Bingo spied his chance. There was no-one coming in, nor was there anyone going out and Mum Dad and Ally were all looking where they were going. Luckily, they were all in such a hurry to get out that no-one had bothered to look round and talk to 'Grandad.'

Bingo grabbed hold of Boggart's sleeve again and closed his eyes tightly.

'Grandad!' exclaimed Mum, turning round just before they reached the door. 'I've only just realised. When you came out of that office you didn't have your walking sti . . .'

Mum's voice trailed off as she realised that she was talking to the empty space where, only a couple of seconds before, 'Grandad' had been walking beside Bingo. 'Where has he gone now?' she said. 'How did you manage to lose him this time, Bingo?'

Bingo, fumbling for his match-box with one hand and gently holding something quite wriggly and tickly in the other, said innocently, 'Who, Mum?'

'Grandad, of course. Don't tell me you've lost him again.'

'Of course I'm not lost,' said a voice from near the door. 'Although I might have been if it had been up to you lot. Fancy going off without me.'

Bingo sighed another of his deep sighs.

The voice belonged to his grandad who had just entered the Gallery.

'How did you get there?' Dad asked.

'On my feet, just like you,' Grandad replied. 'But where have you been?'

Dad looked puzzled. 'We've been in here with you!'

'But I haven't been in there!' said Grandad. 'I've been waiting outside for you until a minute ago when a man came out with a sign saying that the exhibition was cancelled. Before that I was talking to a man in the tobacconists who knew my Uncle Bill who used to take me fishing when I was a lad. He said that Uncle Bill's wife, that's my uncle Bill whose been dead and gone these forty years, used to . . .'

'Never mind that now!' said Mum. 'We must be getting home. Come on. And you've got your walking stick, I see!'

Mum whispered in Dad's ear as they walked down the road, 'It's his age, you know. He's getting very absent-minded.'

Ally and Bingo walked along towards the station and talked about everything under the sun except the Cube.

As they waited for the train, Grandad chatted about the great steam engines which he had seen at that station, many years ago. When the train pulled into the platform Grandad said a very strange thing.

'Do you know,' he said, 'that when I walked into the open door of the Gallery I thought I was walking into a mirror. Either that or I saw myself coming out.'

Grandad pulled out his handkerchief and mopped his brow. 'I think I'll have to start wearing my glasses more often,' he said. 'Can't do with seeing things that aren't there.'

Ally looked very puzzled.

Later that night, in Bingo's bedroom, Boggart was allowed to be his real self for a few minutes before Bingo changed him back into a caterpillar and popped him into the glass jar next to his bed.

'What a time I had!' Boggart giggled softly. 'All that excitement!'

'There was almost too much excitement for me,' declared Bingo as he remembered how sad he had been when he thought that Boggart was lost for ever. 'I thought I'd never see you again, especially when the Attendant took you to the office. How on earth did you talk your way out of that?'

'I was a little bit naughty,' Boggart admitted. 'When they asked me if I had the Cube I didn't know what to say. In one way I did have it but in another way I didn't, so I just said nothing.'

'But you did talk to the men later,' said Bingo. 'We saw you through the office window.'

'Ah!' said Boggart, wagging his finger. 'That was when they asked me who I was.'

Bingo looked horrified. 'And what did you tell them?'

'That was when I was a little bit naughty,' giggled Boggart. 'I remembered you once told me that grown-ups never believe anything magical, so I told them the truth. I said I was a Boggart who used to live under the ground and that if they used a little imagination they could turn me back into the Cube.'

Open mouthed and wide eyed, Bingo stared at his friend.

'And then the men just laughed,' said Boggart seriously. 'They patted me on the shoulder, made me a cup of tea and said "Poor old chap!" I don't really think they believed me.'

'I wonder why not?' Bingo asked as he tried, with difficulty to keep his face straight. 'I wonder why not?'

'I don't know,' replied Boggart wistfully. 'After all, I was famous for a little while and worth an awful lot of money. Did you think I was worth half a million dollars?'

'Boggart!' exclaimed Bingo as he imagined his friend back into the shape of a caterpillar and popped him into the jar beside his bed. 'I think you're priceless!'